Who Can Help?

by Donna Foley

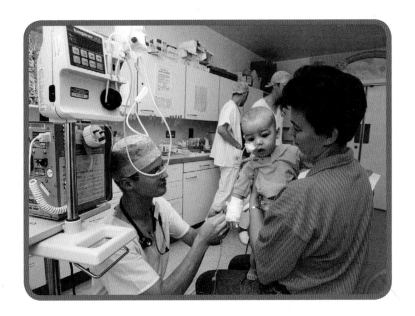

Editorial Offices: Glenview, Illinois • Parsippany, New Jersey • New York, New York
Sales Offices: Needham, Massachusetts • Duluth, Georgia • Glenview, Illinois
Coppell, Texas • Ontario, California • Mesa, Arizona

Every effort has been made to secure permission and provide appropriate credit for photographic material. The publisher deeply regrets any omission and pledges to correct errors called to its attention in subsequent editions.

Unless otherwise acknowledged, all photographs are the property of Scott Foresman, a division of Pearson Education.

Photo locators denoted as follows: Top (T), Center (C), Bottom (B), Left (L), Right (R), Background (Bkgd)

Opener: ©DK Images;1 ©DK Images;3 Getty Images; 4 Getty Images; 5 Getty Images; 6 ©DK Images; 7 Getty Images; 8 ©DK Images; 9 Borkoski, Matthew/Index Stock Imagery; 10 (B) ©DK Images, (C) Tony Freeman/PhotoEdit; 12 ©DK Images; 13 ©DK Images; 15 Getty Images

ISBN: 0-328-13293-4

Copyright © Pearson Education, Inc.

All Rights Reserved. Printed in the United States of America. This publication is protected by Copyright, and permission should be obtained from the publisher prior to any prohibited reproduction, storage in a retrieval system, or transmission in any form by any means, electronic, mechanical, photocopying, recording, or likewise. For information regarding permission(s), write to: Permissions Department, Scott Foresman, 1900 East Lake Avenue, Glenview, Illinois 60025.

8 9 10 V010 14 13 12 11 10 09 08

Community workers include 911 operators, EMTs, firefighters, police officers, nurses, and doctors. They all work together to help people in danger. Together, they keep their community safe. Let's learn about how these community workers make our lives better.

911 Operators

Emergency line operators, or 911 operators, answer phone calls from people in danger. They keep the caller calm and ask the right questions. They make sure help gets sent out **quickly.** The 911 operators make sure that other people on the emergency team know everything they need to know to help.

EMT Workers

An EMT is an emergency medical technician. EMTs pick up sick and hurt people and take them to the hospital. EMTs drive ambulances and get people to the hospital quickly. EMTs make sure people get the best care before a doctor or nurse can see them.

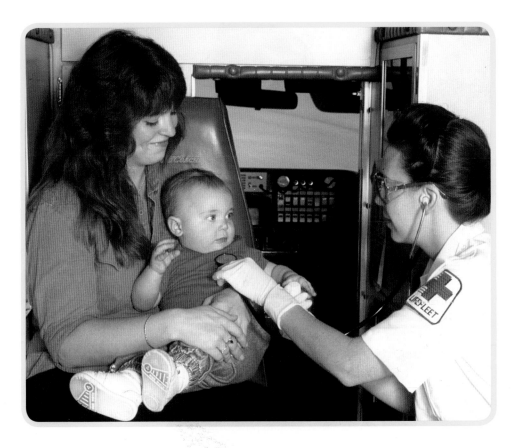

Firefighters

Firefighters help people caught in a fire. They can help people get out of **burning buildings.** Firefighters can save peoples' houses and belongings. Even when there isn't a fire, firefighters can sometimes use their equipment to help people in need.

Police Officers

Police officers serve and protect the people in their communities in many ways. Some police officers stop people from hurting themselves and others. Other police officers make sure drivers are driving safely. Police officers make sure everyone follows the community's rules.

Nurses and Doctors

Nurses usually work in a hospital. They help patients, doctors, and EMTs. They can help care for people who are elderly, sick, or hurt. Nurses make sure doctors get important information. They help people stay safe when the doctor is not around.

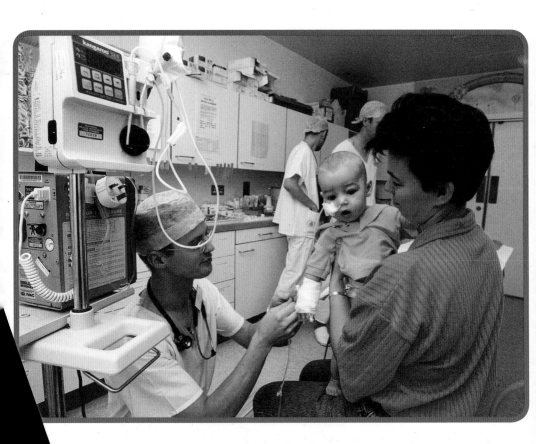

Doctors help people who are sick. Some doctors operate on people who are seriously hurt. Doctors give people medicines that can help cure their illnesses. Doctors also help teach people how to take care of themselves so they can stay healthy.

In an Emergency

All the people you have learned about work together to help people in need. Let's see how they do their jobs in an emergency.

In an emergency a person dials 911. The 911 operator takes the call and finds out what kind of emergency it is.

The 911 operator then calls the police and the fire departments. She gives police officers and firefighters information about the person who needs help.

The 911 operator also has the important job of keeping the caller calm until help arrives.

At the fire **station** the firefighters put on their gear and jump on the fire engine. Their sirens **roar.** The firefighters hold on **tightly.** Once they get to the fire, the firefighters pull out their hoses and spray the fire with water. They need to work quickly to save lives.

The firefighters wear **masks** to protect themselves from the smoke. They put on their masks and enter the burning building. The firefighters carry people out of the building and hand them over to the EMTs. The EMTs check the patients and drive them to the hospital.

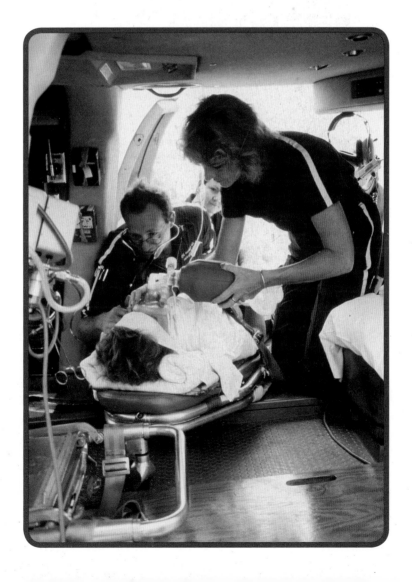

Police also respond to the call for help. They block off traffic to keep other people away from the fire. Police officers help firefighters and EMTs do their work safely. Without police officers keeping things safe, the firefighters and EMTs would have a lot more things to worry about.

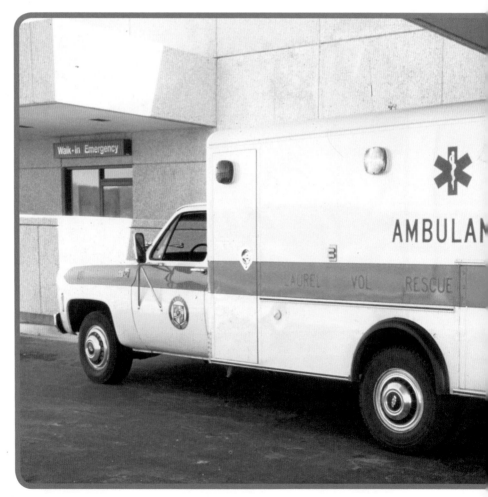

On the way to the hospital, EMTs call the nurses and give them information about what the patients need. Nurses and doctors wait for the ambulance. They rush patients to the emergency room.

Now the community workers have done their jobs. The patients are safe!

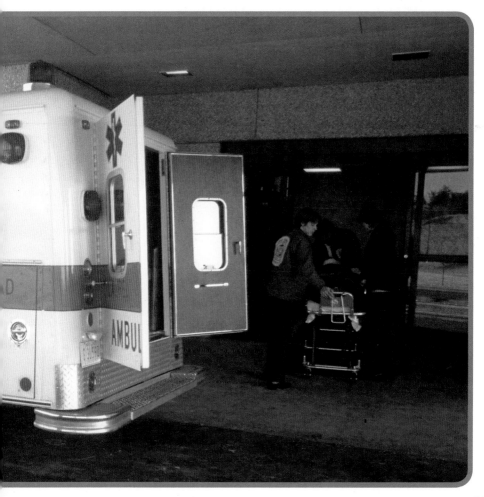

Glossary

buildings *n.* houses, apartments, or places where people live, work, or play.

burning *v.* on fire.

masks *n.* coverings that people wear to protect their faces.

quickly *adv.* with speed.

roar *v.* to make a loud sound like a lion.

station *n.* a central place where people gather.

tightly *adv.* securely.